The

The Gospel of John

A rendering in English by
Kalmia Bittleston

Floris Books

First published by Floris Books in 1984

ISBN 0–86315–012–8

Printed in Great Britain
by Clark Constable, Edinburgh, London, Melbourne

Contents

Jesus makes the journey from the Jordan Valley to Galilee, and back to the Jordan

Jesus journeys to Galilee and then returns to Jerusalem

Jesus in Galilee

Jesus in Jerusalem

Jesus in Bethany and Ephraim

Jesus returns to Bethany and Jerusalem

The Passion

The Resurrection

Introduction

The Gospel of John is written in quite a different style from that of the other three Gospels. It has sometimes been described as a poem, and the layout of this English rendering is that of a dramatic poem. As in all spiritual texts, the repetition is very important, with the stressed word often coming at the end of the line.

Many people know the first verses of the Gospel by heart, and may find this version of the Prologue very difficult. In the Greek text it is immediately apparent that the same verb has been used purposely over and over again; nine times in nineteen verses. Here an attempt has been made to keep to this. Elsewhere this principle has only been followed with a few key words.

In Greek the person speaking, or the person who is being addressed, is usually made clear by the ending of the verb, and is not stated separately. If it is written separately, then a literal translation would be, not just 'I am', but 'I, I am'. There are many such moments in John, and here the pronoun is either written twice; or 'myself', 'himself' or 'yourselves' has been inserted according to the sense. Alternatively, 'indeed' has been added as a means of emphasis. If the double pronoun is found to be difficult to read aloud, then the emphasis can simply be made clear by the voice.

The Fourth Gospel gives a historical framework which is not present in the same way in the synoptics. Three Passovers are mentioned, also the Feast of Tabernacles which was a harvest festival, and the Feast of the Dedication of the Temple, which took place in midwinter. An unnamed festival (John 5) was probably also the Feast of Tabernacles.

As well as the background of the seasons, there is a spiral rhythm in John's Gospel, one of the many rhythms which it would no doubt be possible to find in these ever-living pages.

The Gospel is clearly divided into two halves. The first half, consisting of chapters 1 to 10, begins with the Prologue, continues with 'the witness of John' and ends with another reference to John the Baptist. The second half, chapters 11 to 21, begins with the raising of Lazarus and ends with the resurrection scene by the Sea of Galilee. This second half contains all the references to the disciple whom Jesus loved.

Each of the two halves can again be divided into four spirals. The first spiral consists of chapters 1 to 3, and covers Christ's journey from the Jordan valley to Galilee, and back again to the Jordan, after a visit to Jerusalem for the Passover. In the second, chapters 4 and 5, there is again a journey to Galilee, and back to Jerusalem (Feast of Tabernacles?). The third spiral, chapter 6, takes place entirely in Galilee, just before the Passover, and in the fourth, chapters 7 to 10, Christ goes up to Jerusalem for the Feast of Tabernacles, and is also in Jerusalem at the Feast of the Dedication.

Except for the Epilogue, the second half takes place entirely in Judea. The first spiral, chapter 11, describes the raising of Lazarus. The second, chapters 12 to 17, contains all the farewell talks, from the washing of the feet to the high-priestly prayer; and in the third, chapters 18 and 19, we have the betrayal, trial, crucifixion and burial.

The fourth, last spiral, chapter 20, is the resurrection. Chapter 21, again by the Sea of Galilee, supplies the Epilogue.

Such a consideration of the structure may be a help in getting to know the Gospel; and to know it is the first step towards understanding it, but of the search for understanding there can never be an end.

The Gospel of John

1 *Prologue. The Incarnation*

1 In the Beginning
   Was the Word
   And the Word
   Was with God
   And the Word
   Was God
2 He was in the Beginning
   With God

3 Through him
   Everything entered into existence
   And without him
   Nothing entered into existence

   What existed
4 Was life in him
   And the life was the light of mankind
5 And the light
   Shines in the darkness
   But the darkness
   Has not taken hold of it

6 There entered into existence
   A man sent out from God
   His name was John

7   He came as a witness
To bear witness to the Light
So that everyone
Might believe through him

8   He was not the Light
But should bear witness to the Light
9   The true Light
Who enlightens every human being
Coming into the world

10   He was in the world
Through him the world
Entered into existence
And the world
Was not aware of him

11   He came into his own
And those who were his own
Did not receive him

12   To all who accepted him
He gave the authority
For their existence as children of God

For those who believe in his name
13   It was not of blood-streams
Nor of the will of the flesh
Nor of the will of mortal man
But of God
That they were born

14   In the flesh
The Word entered into existence
And made his dwelling among us
And we beheld the glory of his revelation
Revealed as an only-born from his Father
Full of grace and truth

15   John bears witness to him
And has cried out
This was the one
Of whom I spoke
The one
Who coming after me
Has existed before me
Because he preceded me

16   Out of his fullness
We have all received grace
In the place of grace

17   Because the Law
Was given through Moses
But grace and truth
Entered into existence through Jesus Christ

18   No one has ever had sight of God
The only-born Son
Who is within the being of the Father
He is the interpreter

The witness of John the Baptist

19 And this is the witness of John
When the Jews
Sent out priests and Levites from Jerusalem
So that they could ask him
You
Who are you?

20 He confessed
And did not deny it
But confessed
I
I am not the Christ

21 They asked him
Then are you Elijah?

He said
I am not

Are you the Prophet?

And he answered
No

22 So they said to him
Who are you?
We must give an answer
To those who sent us
What do you say about yourself?

23   He declared
          As a voice
          I call in the desert
          Make straight the way of the Lord
          As was said by the prophet Isaiah

24   Now they had been sent out
      By the Pharisees

25   And they asked him
          Why are you baptizing
          If you are neither the Christ
          Nor Elijah
          Nor the Prophet?

26   John answered them
          I myself baptize in water
          He stands among you
          Whom indeed you do not know
27   He is the one
          Who comes after me
          And I
          I am not worthy
          To undo the strap of his sandal

28   All this took place in Bethany
      Beyond the Jordan
      Where John was baptizing

29   The next day
      He saw Jesus coming towards him

And said
    Look on the Lamb of God
    The bearer of the sin of the world
30   This is he
    Of whom I myself said
    One grown to manhood comes after
      me
    Who existed before me
    Because he preceded me

31   I indeed did not know him
    In order that he should be shown to
      Israel
    I
    I have come
    Baptizing in water

32   And John bore witness
    Thus I beheld the Spirit
    Descending as a dove from heaven
    And remaining on him

33   I indeed did not know him
    But the one who sent me
    To baptize in water
    Is the one who said to me
    He on whom you see the Spirit
      descending
    And remaining on him
    He it is
    Who will baptize in Holy Spirit

34   And I
        I have perceived
        And have borne witness
        That this is the Son of God

The calling of the first disciples
35 On the next day
    John was standing there again
    With two of his disciples
36   And watching Jesus where he walked
            He said
                    Look on the Lamb of God

37 The two disciples
    Heard him speak
    And they followed Jesus

38   Jesus turned
            And beheld them following
            And said to them
                    What do you need?

        And they said to him
                    Rabbi
                    (Which being translated
                    Means teacher)
                    Where are you staying?

39   He said to them
                    Come
                    And you will see

So they came
And saw where he was staying
And remained with him that day
It was about the tenth hour

40 One of the two
Who heard John speak
And then followed Jesus
Was Simon Peter's brother Andrew
41   Who first found his own brother Simon
        Then said to him
            We have found the Messiah
            (Which being translated
            Means Christ)

42 He brought him to Jesus

        Gazing into him
        Jesus said
            You are Simon the son of John
            You shall be called Kephas
            (Which is translated
            Peter)

43 On the next day
He intended to go into Galilee

        Jesus found Philip
        And said to him
            Follow me

44 Now Philip came from Bethsaida
The same town as Andrew and Peter

45 Philip found Nathanael
And told him
We have found the one
Of whom Moses wrote in the Law
And of whom the prophets wrote also
Jesus from Nazareth
The son of Joseph

46 And Nathanael said to him
From Nazareth?
Is it possible for anything that is good
To be from there?

Philip said to him
Come and see

47 Jesus saw Nathanael
Coming to him
And said
Look on a true Israelite
In whom is no deceit

48 Nathanael said to him
How is it that you
Recognize me?

Jesus replied
Before Philip called you

When you were under the fig tree
I saw you

49　Nathanael answered him
Rabbi
You are the Son of God
You are the King of Israel

50　Jesus answered
Do you believe
Because I said to you
That I saw you under the fig tree?
You shall have sight
Of greater things than these

51　And he said to him
Of a certainty I say to you all
You shall have sight of heaven opened
And the angels of God
Ascending and descending
On the Son of Man

2　*The wedding at Cana*
1　On the third day
A wedding took place
At Cana in Galilee
And the mother of Jesus was there
2　Jesus and his disciples
Were invited to the wedding

3   When there was no more wine
          His mother said to Jesus
              They have no wine

4   And Jesus said to her
          This is between me and you
          Woman
          My hour has still not come

5   His mother said to those who were serving
          Do whatever he tells you

6   Now six stone water-jars
     Were standing there
     Intended for the Jewish rites of purification
     Each contained two or three measures

7   Jesus said to them
          Fill the water-jars with water

     And they filled them
     To the brim

8   Then he said to them
          Draw some out now
          And take it to the master of the feast

     So they took it

9   When the master of the feast
     Had tasted the water

Which had now become wine
And did not know
Where it had come from
(But those who were serving knew
Because they had drawn the water)
> The master of the feast called the
> bridegroom

10 > And said to him
>> Every man
>> Serves the best wine first
>> Then a poorer sort
>> After all have drunk deeply
>> But you
>> You have kept the best wine
>> Until now

11 It was at Cana in Galilee
That Jesus performed this sign
The beginning
And manifested the glory of his being
And his disciples believed in him

12 After this
He went down to Capernaum
With his mother
And his brothers
And his disciples
They only remained there
For a few days

Traders expelled from the Temple in Jerusalem

13 It was near the Passover of the Jews
Jesus went up to Jerusalem
14 And found in the Temple
Those who sold oxen
And sheep
And doves
And coin-dealers sitting there

15 He made a lash out of cords
And drove them all out of the Temple
With the sheep
And the oxen
He poured out the money-changers' coins
And overturned their tables

16 Then he said to the ones who sold doves
Take them all away from here
Do not make my Father's house
Into a house for trade

17 The disciples remembered
That it is written
The zeal of thy house
Will eat me up

18 So the Jews replied to him
What sign will you show us
Now that you do such things?

19 Jesus answered
> Break down this temple
> And I will raise it up
> In three days

20 Then the Jews said to him
> It took forty-six years
> To build this temple
> And you
> Will you raise it up
> In three days?

21 But he spoke
About the temple of his body

22 When he was raised from the dead
His disciples remembered
That he had said this
And they believed the Scripture
And the words
Which Jesus had spoken

23 Now when he was in Jerusalem
At the Passover festival
Many believed in his name
Because they perceived the signs
Which he did

24 But Jesus did not trust himself to them
25 Because he understood them all
And did not need anyone

To witness
On behalf of humanity
Because he knew
What was in humanity

3   *The conversation with Nicodemus*

1   Now there was a man of the Pharisees
Whose name was Nicodemus
He was a leader among the Jews

2   He came to Jesus at night
And said to him
Rabbi
We know
That you have come from God
As a teacher
For no one has power to do the signs
Which you are doing
Unless God is with him

3   Jesus answered him
Of a certainty I say to you
Unless someone is born again
He is powerless to see
The kingdom of God

4   Nicodemus said to him
What power has a man
To be born
When he is old?

Has he power to enter his mother's
    womb
For the second time
And be born?

5   Jesus answered
Of a certainty I say to you
Unless someone is born
Out of water and spirit
He is powerless to enter
The kingdom of God
6   Born out of the flesh is flesh
Born out of the spirit is spirit

7   Do not be astonished
Because I said to you
You all must be born again
8   The wind
Blows where it wills
And you hear the sound it makes
But you do not know
Where it comes from
Or where it is going
It is the same with everyone
Born out of the spirit

9   Nicodemus answered
How has this the power
To come about?

10   Jesus answered him
                You yourself are the teacher of Israel
                And yet you do not understand this?

11   Of a certainty I say to you
                It is of what we know
                That we speak
                And to what we have seen
                We bear witness
                And you all
                Do not receive our witness

12   If I have spoken to you all
                About the concerns of earth
                And you do not believe
                If I speak to you all
                About the concerns of heaven
                Will you believe?

13   No-one
                Has gone up into heaven
                Except the one
                Who has come down out of heaven
                The Son of Man
                [Who is in heaven]

14   Just as Moses
                Lifted up the serpent in the desert
                The Son of Man
                Must be lifted up
15   So that everyone who believes in him

May live
Throughout the ages

16   Because God so loved the world
That he gave the Son
Born the only one
So that everyone who believes in
   him
Should not be destroyed
But live
Throughout the ages

17   Because God did not send the Son
Out into the world
To pass sentence on the world
But so that the world
Might be saved through him

18   If anyone believes in him
He is not brought to judgment
If anyone does not believe
He has been condemned already
Because he did not believe
In the name
Of the only one
Born Son of God

19   And this is the judgment
That the light
Has come into the world
And men loved darkness

Rather than light
Because their deeds were evil

20 All those who practise meanness
Hate the light
And do not come to the light
So that their deeds are not shamed
21 All those who do what is true
Come to the light
So that their deeds may be shown
To be performed in God

The confession of John the Baptist
22 After these events
Jesus and his disciples
Came into the land of Judea
And he stayed there with them
And baptized

23 John was also baptizing
In Ainon near Salem
Where water was plentiful
The people came there
And were baptized
24 Because John
Had not yet been thrown into prison

25 Now there was a discussion
Between John's disciples
And a Jew
About purification

26   They came to John
       And said to him
            Rabbi
            The one who was with you
            Beyond the Jordan
            And to whom you bore witness
            Look how he is baptizing
            And everyone comes to him

27   John answered
            A man has no power to receive
                anything
            Unless it is given to him from heaven
28   You yourselves bear me witness
            That I said
            I
            I am not the Christ
            But I have been sent out before him

29   The one who has the bride
            Is the bridegroom
            But the bridegroom's friend
            Who stands and hears him
            Is filled with joy
            And rejoices
            Because of the bridegroom's voice
            So now
            My joy is complete

30 He must wax
But I must wane
31 The one who comes from above
Is over all
He who is earthly
Belongs to the earth
And speaks about the earth
The one who comes from heaven
Is over all

32 He bears witness
To what he has seen
And to what he has heard
And no-one accepts his witness
33 Whoever accepts his witness
Puts his seal
To the truth of God

34 He whom God has sent out
Speaks God's words
Because it is not only in verse metre
That the Spirit is given

35 The Father loves the Son
And has given everything
Into his hand

36 He who believes in the Son
Has life
Throughout the ages
He who does not obey the Son

Will not have sight of life
But the anger of God
Remains upon him

4   *The conversation with a Samaritan woman*

1   Now when the Lord knew
That the Pharisees had heard
That Jesus
Is making more disciples than John
And is baptizing them

2   Although Jesus himself
Did not baptize
But his disciples did so

3   He left Judea
And returned to Galilee

4   He had to pass through Samaria

5   And came to a Samaritan town
Called Sychar
Near the land given by Jacob
To his son Joseph

6   Jacob's spring was there
As Jesus was tired from the journey
He sat straight down by the spring
It was about the sixth hour

7   A Samaritan woman
Came to draw water

Jesus said to her
   Give me a drink

8 His disciples
  Had gone away into the town
  To buy food

9   The Samaritan woman said to him
      As you are a Jew
      How can you ask me
      For a drink
      As I am a woman
      And a Samaritan

Because Jews handle nothing
In common with Samaritans

10   Jesus answered her
      If you knew the gift of God
      And who it is
      That is saying to you
      Give me a drink
      You would have asked him
      And he would have given to you
      Living water

11   She said to him
      Sir
      You have no water-bucket
      And the well is deep
      From where do you have

The living water?
12 Surely you are not greater
Than our father Jacob
Who gave us the well
And drank from it himself
As did his sons
And his cattle?

13 Jesus answered her
Everyone who drinks this water
Will be thirsty again
14 But whoever drinks the water
Which I myself will give him
Will never be thirsty again
Because the water
Which I will give him
Will become in him
A spring of water
Welling up as a source of life
Throughout the ages

15 The woman said to him
Sir
Give me this water
So that I am not thirsty
And need not come here
To draw it

16 He said to her
Go and call your husband
And come here

17   The woman answered
      I have no husband

    Jesus said to her
      It is right when you say
      I have no husband
18   Because you have had five husbands
      And he whom you have now
      Is not your husband
      In this you spoke the truth

19   The woman said to him
      Sir
      I perceive that you are a prophet
20   Our fathers worshipped
      In this mountain
      And you all say
      That in Jerusalem
      Is the place where there should be
        worship

21   Jesus said to her
      Believe me
      Woman
      The hour is coming
      When neither in this mountain
      Nor in Jerusalem
      Will you all worship the Father

22   What you worship
      You do not know

What we worship
We know
Because salvation
Comes from the Jews

23   But the hour is coming
And has come now
When the true worshippers
Will worship the Father
In spirit and in truth
For indeed the Father
Seeks such people to worship him

24   God is spirit
And those who worship
In spirit and in truth
Must they worship

25   The woman said to him
I know
That Messiah is coming
He who is called Christ
When he comes
He will make everything clear to us

26   Jesus said to her
I
I AM
The one who is speaking to you

27 And at this
His disciples came
And were astonished
That he was talking to a woman
But no one said
What do you need?
Or
Why are you talking to her?

28 Then the woman
Left her water-jar
And went into the town
And said to the men
29 Come and see a man
Who told me everything
That I have done
Is not this the Christ?

30 They went out of the town
And came to him

31 In the meantime
His disciples said to him
Rabbi
Eat

32 But he said to them
I myself have food to eat
About which you know nothing

33   So the disciples said to one another
                Has anyone
                Brought him something to eat?

34   Jesus said to them
                My food
                Is to do the will
                Of the one who sent me
                And to complete his work

35   Do you not have a saying
                There are still four months
                And then comes the harvest?
                I tell you to look
                And lift up your eyes
                And behold the fields
                Because they are white
                Ready for the harvest

36   Already the reaper receives wages
                And gathers fruit
                For life
                Throughout the ages
                So that sower and reaper
                May rejoice together

37   For in this
                The saying is true
                That one sows and another reaps
38   I myself sent you out to reap
                Where indeed you did not toil

Others have toiled
And you
You have entered into their toil

39 Many Samaritans
From that town
Believed in him
Because of the woman's words
Which bore witness
He told me
All that I had done

40 So when the Samaritans
Came to him
They asked him to remain with them
And he remained with them
For two days
41 And many more believed
Because of his word

42 And they said to the woman
We no longer believe
Because of what you said
But we believe
Because we have heard for ourselves
And we know
That this is truly
The Saviour of the world

The healing of a courtier's son

43 After two days
He left there
And went into Galilee

44 For Jesus
Had himself borne witness
That a prophet has no honour
In his own native place

45 So when he came into Galilee
The Galileans welcomed him
Because they had seen
All that he had done
At the festival in Jerusalem
They had also been to the festival

46 Then he came to Cana in Galilee again
Where he had made the water wine

When a courtier
Whose son was ill in Capernaum
47 Heard that Jesus
Had come to Galilee from Judea
He went to him
And asked him to come down
And heal his son
Who was about to die

48   Jesus said to him
        Unless you all see signs and portents
        You will not believe

49   The courtier said to him
        Sir
        Come down
        Before my little child dies

50   Jesus said to him
        Go
        Your son lives

The man believed the word
Which Jesus had said to him
And he went

51   As he was returning
His servants met him
And told him that his boy lives
52   So he asked them
At what time he began to improve
        They said to him
            Yesterday
            At the seventh hour
            The fever left him

53   Then the father became aware
That it was at the very hour
In which Jesus had said to him
Your son lives

And he believed
As did his whole household

54 Now this was the second sign
Performed by Jesus
When he had come to Galilee from Judea

5 *The healing at the Pool of Bethesda*
1 After this there was a Jewish festival
And Jesus went up to Jerusalem

2 Now in Jerusalem
There is a pool which has five colonnades
It is near the Sheep Gate
And in Hebrew it is called Bethesda

3 Many disabled people were lying there
The blind
The lame
And the paralysed

[They were waiting for the water to be moved
4 Because at certain times
An angel went down into the pool
And stirred up the water
Whoever stepped in first
After the water was disturbed
Was made whole from his disability]

5 There was one man
   Who had been disabled
   For thirty-eight years

6 When Jesus saw him
   And became aware
   That he had been lying there
   For a long time
        He said to him
            Is it your will
            To become whole?

7   The one who was disabled
       Answered him
            Sir
            I do not have a man
            To drop me into the pool
            When the water is disturbed
            But while I
            I am coming
            Someone else goes down before me

8   Jesus said to him
            Rise
            Take up your mat
            And walk

9 At once
   The man became whole
   Took up his mat
   And walked

And that day was the sabbath

10   Therefore the Jews
        Said to the one who was cured
            It is the sabbath
            You are not allowed
            To carry your mat

11   But he answered them
            He who made me whole
            Said to me
            Take up your mat
            And walk

12   They asked him
            Who is the man
            Who said to you
            Take it up and walk?

13 But the one who had been healed
    Did not know who it was
    As Jesus had withdrawn
    In that crowded place

14   Afterwards Jesus found him in the Temple
        And said to him
            See
            You have become whole
            Do not sin any more
            Or something worse may befall you

15   The man went away
      And told the Jews
      That it was Jesus
      Who had made him whole
16   Therefore the Jews persecuted Jesus
      Because he did such things
      On a sabbath

17   But he answered them
              My Father is still working now
              And I myself am working

18   For this reason the Jews
      Were all the more anxious to kill him
      Because he not only broke the sabbath
      But called God his own Father
      Making himself equal with God

Jesus answers the Jews
19   So Jesus said to them
              Of a certainty I say to you
              The son has no power
              To do anything out of himself
              Except what he sees
              The Father doing
              For whatever he does
              The Son does also

20   Because the Father
              Cares for the Son
              And shows him everything

That he is doing
And he will show him
Greater deeds than these
So that even you
May be astonished

21 Just as the Father
Raises the dead
And gives them life
So the Son also gives life
To those to whom he will

22 The Father judges no one
But has given all judgment to the Son
23 So that everyone should reverence the
Son
As much as they reverence the Father
He who does not reverence the Son
Lacks reverence for the Father
Who sent him

24 Of a certainty I say to you
Whoever hears my words
And believes in the one who sent me
· Will live
Throughout the ages
And will not come to the parting of
the ways
But has passed out of death
Into life

25 Of a certainty I say to you
 The hour has now come
 When the dead
 Will hear the voice of the Son of God
 And those who hear will live

26 Just as the Father
 Bears life within himself
 He has given to the Son
 To bear life within himself
27 And he has given him authority
 To make a division
 Because he is Son of Man

28 Do not be astonished at this
 Because the hour is coming
 When all those who are in the graves
 Will hear his voice
29 And will come out
 Those who have done good
 To a resurrection of life
 Those who have practised meanness
 To a resurrection of condemnation

30 For I
 I have no power
 To do anything out of myself
 As I hear I judge
 And my judgment is just
 Because it is not my aim
 To carry out my own will

But the will
Of the one who sent me

31 If I
I bear witness to myself
Then my evidence
Is not accepted as the truth
32 There is someone else
Who gives evidence about me
And I know
That the evidence which he gives
 about me
Is the truth
33 You yourselves sent out to John
And he bore witness
To the truth

34 Indeed I
I do not receive the testimony of
 men
But I say this
So that you yourselves may be saved
35 He was a lamp
Burning and shining
And for a while
Even you were willing
To rejoice in his light

36 But I
I have a greater witness
Than that of John

As the deeds which the Father
Gave me to complete
These deeds which I am doing
Are evidence that the Father
Has sent me out

37 And the Father who sent me
Has borne witness to me
You have never heard his voice
You have not perceived his form
38 And his word does not remain in you
Because you
You do not believe
The one whom he has sent out

39 You study the Scriptures
Which bear witness to me
Because you think that in them
You have the life
Which endures throughout the ages
40 But you will not come to me
So that you may have life

41 I do not accept the esteem of men
42 But I know
That you do not have within you
The love of God

43 I
I have come in my Father's name
And you do not accept me

If someone else comes in his own
    name
You will accept him

44   How indeed have you the power to
    believe
Who accept the esteem of one another
And do not aim for the esteem of the
    only God

45   Do not think that I
I will accuse you to the Father
There is someone else who accuses
    you
And that is Moses
In whom you hoped

46   Because if you had believed Moses
You would have believed me
For he wrote about me

47   But if you do not believe what he has
    written
How will you believe my words?

6   *The feeding of the five thousand*

1   After these events
Jesus went away
Across the Sea of Galilee
Which is the Sea of Tiberias

2   And a great crowd followed him
Because they saw the signs
Which he had done
For those who were disabled

3   Jesus went up on to the mountain
       And sat there with his disciples

4   It was near the Passover
       A festival of the Jews

5   Jesus lifted up his eyes
       And beholding the crowds
       Coming towards him
           He said to Philip
               Where should we buy bread
               For these people to eat?

6   He said this to test him
       Because he knew
       What he was going to do

7   Philip answered him
               Two hundred denarii
               Would not buy enough bread
               For each one to take a little

8   Andrew
           Simon Peter's brother
           Who was one of his disciples
           Said to him
9   There is a child here
               He has five barley loaves
               And two little fishes
               But what is this
               Among so many?

10   Jesus said
          Make the people sit down

Now there was plenty of grass there
So the men sat down
They numbered about five thousand

11   Then Jesus took the loaves
And when he had given thanks
He passed them over
To those sitting down
And the same with the fish
As much as they wished

12   When they were satisfied
        He said to his disciples
            Collect the pieces left over
            So that nothing is destroyed

13   They gathered them up
And filled twelve baskets
With pieces of the five barley loaves
Which had been left over
By those who had eaten

14   When the people
      Saw the sign which he had done
      They said
          This is in truth the prophet
          The one coming into the world

15 Then Jesus was aware
That they were about to come
And carry him off
To make him a king
So he went away again
On to the mountain
Himself alone

The disciples see Jesus walking on the water
16 When it grew late
His disciples went down to the sea
17 They embarked in a boat
And set out across the sea
Towards Capernaum

Although it was now dark
Jesus had not yet come to them
18 And the sea became rough
Because a strong wind was blowing

19 So when they had rowed
About twenty-five or thirty stadia
They perceived Jesus
Walking on the sea
And drawing near the boat
And they were afraid

20   But he said to them
    I
    I AM
    Do not be afraid

21   Then they were willing
To take him into the boat
And immediately the boat
Was at the land to which they were going

The sermon in Capernaum on the bread of life
22   The next day
The crowd which had remained
Over the sea
Discovered that only one small boat
Had been there
And that Jesus
Had not entered the boat with his disciples
But that his disciples
Had gone away alone
23   Although other small boats from Tiberias
Came near the place
Where they had eaten bread
After the Lord had given thanks

24   So when the crowd
Saw that Jesus was not there
Neither were his disciples
Then they also embarked in the boats
And came to Capernaum
Looking for Jesus

25   When they found him
Over the sea
      They said to him

Rabbi
When did you come here?

26 Jesus answered them
Of a certainty I say to you
It is not because you saw signs
That you are looking for me
But because you ate the bread
And were satisfied

27 Do not labour
For the food which perishes
But for the food which remains
As life
Throughout the ages
Which the Son of Man
Will give to you
Because he is the one
Sealed by the Father God

28 Then they said to him
What must we do
So that our deeds
May be God's work?

29 Jesus said to them
This is God's work
That you believe in the one
Whom he has sent out

30   So they said to him
       What sign will you perform
       So that we can see it
       And believe you?
       What are you doing?
31   Our fathers ate manna
       In the desert
       As it is written
       He gave them bread from heaven to eat

32   Therefore Jesus said to them
       Of a certainty I say to you
       It is not Moses
       Who has given you bread from heaven
       But my Father
       Gives you the true bread from heaven
33   Because the bread of God
       Is coming down from heaven
       And giving life to the world

34   Then they said to him
       Sir
       Always give us this bread

35   Jesus said to them
       I
       I AM the bread of life
       He who comes to me
       Will not hunger
       He who believes in me
       Will never thirst

36 But as I told you
You have seen me
And do not believe

37 All that the Father gives to me
Will come to me
And he who comes to me
I will not cast out

38 Because I have not come down from
  heaven
To do my own will
But the will
Of the one who sent me

39 And this is the will
Of the one who sent me
That I should lose nothing
Of all that he has given to me
But should raise it up
At the ending of time

40 For this is the will of my Father
That everyone who looks on the Son
And believes in him
May have life
Throughout the ages
And I myself will raise him up
At the ending of time

41 For this reason
The Jews murmured about him

Because he said
I
I AM the bread
Which has come down from heaven

42   And they said
          Is not this Jesus
          The son of Joseph
          Of whom indeed we know
          The father and the mother?
          How can he now say
          I have come down from heaven?

43   Jesus answered them
          Do not murmur among yourselves
44   No one can come to me
          Unless he is drawn by the Father
          Who sent me
          And I myself
          Will raise him up
          At the ending of time

45   It is written in the prophets
          And they shall all be taught by God

          Everyone who hears
          And learns from the Father
          Comes to me
46   Not that anyone has seen the Father
          Except the one who is with God
          He has seen the Father

47   Of a certainty I say to you
      He who believes
      Has life
      Throughout the ages
48   I
      I AM the bread of life

49   Your fathers ate manna
      In the desert
      And they have died
50   This is the bread
      Which comes down from heaven
      So that anyone may eat it
      And not die

51   I
      I AM the living bread
      Which has come down from heaven
      If anyone eats this bread
      He will live
      Throughout the ages
      And the bread
      Which I will give
      For the life of the world
      Is my flesh

52 Then the Jews
    Argued with one another and said
        How can this man
        Give us his flesh to eat?

53   So Jesus said to them
        Of a certainty I say to you
        Unless you eat the flesh
        Of the Son of Man
        And drink his blood
        You have no life in you
54   He who partakes of my flesh
        And drinks my blood
        Has life
        Throughout the ages
        And I myself
        Will raise him up
        At the ending of time

55   For my flesh is true food
        And my blood is true drink
56   He who partakes of my flesh
        And drinks my blood
        Remains in me
        And I
        I remain in him

57   As the living Father
        Has sent me out
        And I myself live
        Because of the Father
        He who partakes of me
        Will also live
        Because of me

58   This is the bread
        Which has come down from heaven
        Unlike the fathers
        Who ate and died
        He who partakes of this bread
        Will live
        Throughout the ages

59 He said this in synagogue
   Teaching in Capernaum

The difficulties of the disciples

60   When they heard this
        Many of his disciples said
            These are difficult words
            Who can accept them?

61 But within himself Jesus knew
   That his disciples murmured about this
      And he said to them
         Does this offend you?

62   What then if you perceive the Son of
          Man
        Ascending to where he was before?

63   It is the spirit that gives life
        The flesh is of no benefit
        The words
        Which I myself have spoken to you
        They are spirit
        And are life

64   And some of you
     Do not believe

From the beginning
Jesus knew
Who did not believe
And who would betray him

65   And he said
         Therefore I have told you
         That no one can come to me
         Unless it is given to him
         By the Father

66   After this
Many of his disciples turned back
And no longer went about with him

67   So Jesus said to the twelve
         Do not you
         You also wish to go?

68   Simon Peter answered him
         Lord
         To whom should we go?
         You have the words of life
         Which endure throughout the ages
69   And we have come to believe
         And to know
         That you are indeed
         The Holy One of God

70   Jesus answered them
            Did not I myself choose you
            The twelve?
            And one of you is a devil

71   Now he spoke of Judas
     Son of Simon Iscariot
     One of the twelve
     Who was going to betray him

7   *The Feast of Tabernacles*
1   And after these events
     Jesus walked in Galilee
     He would not go about in Judea
     Because the Jews
     Were looking for an opportunity to kill him

2   It was near the Feast of Tabernacles
     A festival of the Jews

3   So his brothers said to him
            Leave here
            And go into Judea
            Then your disciples
            Will be able to see
            The deeds which you perform
4   Because no one
            Does anything in secret
            Who wishes to come into the open
            If you do these things
            Show yourself to the world

5   For even his brothers
Did not believe in him

6   Therefore Jesus said to them
           For me
           The right moment has not yet arrived
           But for you
           It is always the right moment

7   The world
           Has no power to hate you
           But it hates me
           Because I
           I bear witness
           That its deeds are evil

8   Go up yourselves to the festival
           I am not going up myself to this
             festival
           Because for me
           The moment is not ripe

9   After saying this to them
He remained in Galilee
10   But when his brothers
Had gone up to the festival
Then he went up also
Not showing himself
But as if in secret

11   This was the reason why the Jews
    Searched for him at the festival
    And said
        Where is he?

12   And among the crowds
    There was a great deal of murmuring about
       him

        Some said
            He is a good man
        But others said
            No
            He misleads the people

13   But no one spoke about him openly
    Because they were afraid of the Jews

Jesus teaches the crowds in the Temple

14   About half-way through the festival
    Jesus went up into the Temple
    And taught

15   The Jews were astonished
    And said
        How can he understand
        What is written
        As he has never studied?

16   So Jesus answered them
        My teaching is not mine
        But is from the one who sent me
17   If anyone
        Desires to do his will
        He will know
        Whether the teaching comes from
           God
        Or whether I
        I speak out of myself

18   He who speaks out of himself
        Is looking for his own glory
        But he who would give glory
        To the one who sent him
        He is true
        And there is no falsehood in him

19   Did not Moses
        Give you the Law?
        Yet not one of you keeps the Law
        Why do you intend to kill me?

20   The crowd answered
        You have a demon
        Who is intending to kill you?

21   Jesus answered
        I performed one deed
        And you are all astonished

22   Because Moses
Has given you circumcision
(Not that it comes from Moses
But from the Fathers)
You circumcise a man
On a sabbath

23   If a man receives circumcision
On a sabbath
So that the Law of Moses
Is not broken
Why are you angry with me
Because I made the whole of a man
       well
On a sabbath?

24   Do not judge by appearances
But come to a just judgment

25   Then some of the people of Jerusalem said
Is not this the one
Whom they plan to kill?

26   But see how he speaks openly
And they say nothing to him
Surely the rulers have not decided
That he is the Christ?

27   Because we know
From where he is
But when the Christ comes
No one will understand
From where he is

28   Jesus was then teaching in the Temple
And he cried out
     You know me
     And you also know
     From where I am
     I have not come of myself
     But the one who has sent me
     Is true
     Whom you yourselves
     Do not know

29   But I
     I know him
     Because it is from him
     That I AM
     And he is the one
     Who sent me out

30   Then they tried to arrest him
But no one laid hands on him
Because his hour
Had not yet come

31   But many of the crowd
Believed in him
And said
     When the Christ comes
     Surely he will not perform more signs
     Than this one has done?

The attempt to arrest Jesus

32 The Pharisees heard the crowd
Murmuring such things about him
And the chief priests and the Pharisees
Sent out attendants to arrest him

33   Then Jesus said
           For a short time
           I shall still be with you
           Then I am going
           To the one who sent me
34   You will search for me
           And will not find me
           And where I
           I am
           You yourselves
           Have no power to come

35   So then the Jews said to one another
           Where is he about to go
           That we shall not find him?
           Surely he is not going
           To those dispersed among the Greeks
           Or to teach the Greeks?

36   What is the meaning
           Of the words which he said
           You will search for me
           And will not find me
           And where I
           I am

>   You yourselves
>   Have no power to come?

37   Now on the last day
     The great day of the festival
>   Jesus stood and cried out
>   If any one is thirsty
>   Let him come to me
>   And he who believes in me
>   Let him drink
38   As the Scripture has said
>   Out of his body
>   Shall flow rivers of living water

39   But he said this
     Concerning the Spirit
     Whom those who believed in him
     Were to receive
     For not yet was the Spirit present
     Because Jesus was not yet glorified

40   On hearing these words
>   Some of the crowd said
>   This is in truth the prophet

41   Others said
>   This is the Christ

>   Yet others said
>   Surely Christ
>   Will not come from Galilee

42   Has not the Scripture said
            That Christ will come
            From the descendants of David
            And from Bethlehem
            The town of David?

43   Because of him
      The crowd was divided
44   And some wanted to arrest him
      But no one laid hands on him

The Pharisees and Nicodemus
45   Then the attendants
      Came to the chief priests
      And to the Pharisees
            Who said to them
                  Why have you not brought him?

46   The attendants answered
                  No man has ever spoken
                  In the way this man speaks

47   So the Pharisees replied to them
                  Surely you yourselves
48   Have not also been deceived?
                  Have any of the rulers
                  Or of the Pharisees
                  Believed in him?
49   But these people are under a curse
                  Who do not understand the Law

50 One of them was that same Nicodemus
Who had come to Jesus before
And he said to them
51 Does our Law judge a man
Without hearing him first
And understanding what he is doing?

52 They answered him
Surely you yourself
Are not also from Galilee?
Search and you will see
That no prophet
Arises out of Galilee

The adulterous woman
53 [And each one went to his own house
8 But Jesus went to the Mount of Olives

2 At dawn
He returned to the Temple again
And all the people came to him
And sitting down
He taught them

3 Then the scribes and Pharisees
Led in a woman
Who had been taken in adultery
And standing her in the centre
4 They said to him
Teacher
This woman has been caught

In the act of adultery
5 In the Law
Moses commanded us
To stone such a person
What do you say?

6 They said this
In order to test him
So that they might have something
With which to accuse him

But Jesus bent down
And wrote with his finger
In the earth
7 Then as they continued to question him
He stood up

And said to them
The one among you
Who is without sin
Let him be the first
To cast a stone at her

8 And stooping down again
He wrote in the earth

9 When they heard this
They went out one by one
Beginning with the older ones
And he was left alone
With the woman remaining in the centre

10   Standing erect
Jesus said to her
    Where are they?
    Has no one condemned you?

11   And she said
    No one
    Sir

Jesus said
    Neither do I myself
    Condemn you
    Go
    And from now on
    Sin no more]

The light of the world

12   Jesus said to them again
    I
    I AM the light of the world
    He who follows me
    Will not walk in darkness
    But will have the light of life

13   So the Pharisees said to him
    Your testimony
    Is about yourself
    Your evidence
    Cannot be accepted as the truth

14 Jesus answered
    Even if I
    I bear witness about myself
    My evidence is true
    Because I know
    Where I come from
    And where I am going
    But you
    You do not know
    Either where I come from
    Or where I am going

15 You indeed
    Judge according to the flesh
    I bring no one to trial
16 But if I
    I make a division
    My judgment is true
    Because I am not alone
    But with me is the Father
    Who sent me

17 And even in your Law
    It is written
    That the evidence of two men
    Can be accepted as the truth

18 I
    I am the one
    Who bears witness about myself
    And testimony concerning me

Gives the Father
Who sent me

19 Then they said to him
Where is your Father?

Jesus answered them
You neither know me
Nor my Father
If you had known me
You would also have known my
Father

20 He spoke these words in the treasury
Teaching in the Temple
But no one laid hold of him
Because his hour
Had not yet come

A warning to the Jews
21 Then he said to them again
Indeed I am going away
And you will search for me
And in your sin you will die
Where I
I am going
You yourselves
Have not the power to come

22 So then the Jews said
Surely he will not kill himself

Because he says
Where I
I am going
You yourselves
Have not the power to come

23   And he said to them
You
You are from below
I
I am from above
You
You are of this world
I
I am not of this world
24   Therefore I said to you
That you will die in your sins
For if you do not believe
That I
I AM
You will die in your sins

25   Then they said to him
Who are you?

Jesus said to them
THE BEGINNING

But why am I speaking to you?
26   About you I have much to say
And to judge

But the one who sent me is true
And what I myself heard from him
All this I say in the world

27 They did not understand
That he was speaking to them
About the Father

28 So Jesus said
When you have lifted up
The Son of Man
Then you will know
That I
I AM

I do nothing out of myself
But I speak
As the Father taught me
29 And the one who sent me
Is with me
He has not left me alone
Because I
I always do what pleases him

30 As he said all this
Many believed in him

Jesus and Abraham
31 Then Jesus said to those Jews
Who had believed in him
If you yourselves continue in my word

You are truly my disciples
32　And you will know the truth
And the truth will set you free

33　They answered him
We are descendants of Abraham
And have never been the slaves of
anyone
Then how can you say
You will be set free?

34　Jesus answered
Of a certainty I say to you
That every one who sins
Is the slave of sin
35　But the slave
Does not remain in the house
Throughout the ages
The Son remains throughout the ages
36　Therefore if the Son
Sets you free
Free you will be indeed

37　I know
That you are descendants of Abraham
But you want to kill me
Because my word
Finds no space in you

38　What I
I have seen with my Father

I say
What you
You have heard from your father
You do

39
    They answered him
        Abraham is our father

Jesus said to them
    If you were Abraham's children
    You would do as Abraham did
40
    But now you want to kill me
    A man who has told you the truth
    Which I have heard from God
    This Abraham did not do
41
    You
    You do as your father did

They said to him
    We were not born outside the law
    We have only one father
    And that is God

42
Jesus said to them
    If God was your father
    You would have loved me
    Because I
    I came forth
    And have come from God
    I have not come of myself
    But he has sent me

43   Why do you not understand
My way of speaking?
It is because you are powerless
To hear my words

44   You belong to your father
The devil
And wish to carry out
The desires of your father
He was a murderer
From the beginning
And was not grounded in the truth
Because in him there is no truth
When he tells a lie
He speaks out of his own being
Because he is a liar
And the father of it

45   But because I myself tell the truth
You do not believe me
46   Which of you convicts me of sin?
If I tell the truth
Why indeed do you not believe me?

47   A man of God
Hears the words of God
Therefore you yourselves do not hear
Because you are not men of God

48   The Jews answered him
Do not we indeed say rightly

That you
You are a Samaritan
And have a demon?

49   Jesus answered
        I
        I do not have a demon
        But I honour my Father
        And you
        You dishonour me
50   I
        I do not look for my own glory
        There is one who seeks for it
        And who judges of it

51   Of a certainty I say to you
        If anyone keeps my word
        He will not encounter death
        Throughout the ages

52 The Jews said to him
        Now it is clear to us
        That you have a demon
        Abraham died
        And the prophets
        And yet you are saying
        If any one keeps my word
        He will not taste death
        Throughout the ages
53   Surely you are not greater
        Than our father Abraham

Who died
And the prophets who died?
Whom do you make yourself?

54 Jesus answered
But if I
I reveal my being
My revelation is worth nothing
It is my Father
Who reveals my being
Of whom you yourselves say
He is our God

55 You have not understood him
But I
I know him
If I say that I do not know him
I shall be a liar like yourselves
But I know him
And I keep his word

56 Your father Abraham
Rejoiced that he would see my day
And he saw it and was glad

57 Then the Jews said to him
You are not yet fifty years old
And have you seen Abraham?

58 Jesus said to him
Of a certainty I say to you

Before Abraham was
I
I AM

59 Then they took up stones to throw at him
But Jesus hid himself
And went out of the Temple

9 *The healing of the man born blind*
1 And as he passed by
He saw a man
Who had been blind from his birth

2 And his disciples asked him
Rabbi
Was it he or his parents who sinned
Causing him to be born blind?

3 Jesus answered
Neither he nor his parents have sinned
It is so
That the deeds of God within him
May appear outwardly

4 While it is day
We must do the deeds
Of the one who sent me
The night is coming
When no one has the power to work
5 As long as I am in the world
I am the light of the world

6   Having said this
       He spat on the ground
       And made clay of the spittle
       And spread the clay on his eyes
7   And said to him
                Go and wash in the Pool of Siloam
                (Which means
                Having been sent)

       So he went and washed
       And came back seeing

8   Then the neighbours
            And those people
            Who were used to noticing him as a beggar
            Said
                Surely this is not the one
                Who sat and begged?

9   Some said
            It is the one

       Others said
            No
            But he is like him

       He said
            I
            I am

10 So they said to him
How were your eyes opened?

11 He answered them
The man named Jesus
Made clay
And spread it on my eyes
And said to me
Go to Siloam and wash
So I went and washed
And I could see

12 And they said to him
Where is he?

He said
I do not know

13 Then they led the one who had been blind
To the Pharisees

14 The day on which Jesus made clay
And opened his eyes
Was a sabbath

15 Then the Pharisees
Asked him again
How it was that he could see

And he said to them
He spread clay on my eyes

And I washed
And I can see

16   Then some of the Pharisees said
          This man has not come from God
          Because he does not keep the sabbath

But others said
          How has a sinful man
          The power to perform such signs?

And they were divided
Among themselves

17   Again they said
      To the one who was blind
          What do you say about him
          Because he has opened your eyes?

And he said
          He is a prophet

18   But the Jews did not believe
      That he had been blind
      And now could see
      Until they called the parents
      Of the one who now had sight
19   And asked them
               Is this your son
               Whom you say was born blind?
               Then how can he see now?

20 So his parents answered
    We know
    That this is our son
    And that he was born blind
21   But we do not know
    Why he can see now
    Or who opened his eyes
    Ask him
    He is of age
    He will speak for himself

22 His parents said this
Because they were afraid of the Jews
For the Jews had already agreed
That if anyone
Acknowledged him to be Christ
He should be expelled from synagogue
23 Therefore his parents said
He is of age
Question him

24 Then they called
The man who had been born blind
For the second time
And said to him
    Give glory to God
    We know
    That this man is sinful

25   But he answered
            I do not know
            Whether he is sinful
            But one thing I know
            That having been blind
            Now I can see

26   Then they said to him
            What did he do to you?
            How did he open your eyes?

27   He answered them
            I already told you
            And you did not hear
            Why do you wish to hear it again?
            Surely you yourselves have no desire
            To become his disciples?

28   And they abused him
        And said
            You are his disciple
            But we
            We are disciples of Moses
29   For indeed we know
            That God has spoken through Moses
            As for this fellow
            We do not know
            Where he comes from

30   The man answered them
            It is remarkable
            That you do not know
            Where he comes from
            And yet he opened my eyes

31   We know
            That God does not hear the sinful
            But that he hears
            Those who are worshippers of God
            And do his will

32   Throughout the ages
            It has never been heard
            That anyone opened the eyes
            Of the born blind
33   If he did not come from God
            He could do nothing

34   They answered him
            You
            You were entirely born in sin
            And you
            You teach us

     And they threw him out

35   Jesus heard
     That they had thrown him out
     And when he found him
            He said

Do you
In yourself
Believe in the Son of Man?

36   He answered
And who is he
Sir
So that I could believe in him?

37   Jesus said to him
You have seen him
And he is speaking to you

38   Then he declared
Lord
I believe

And he worshipped him

39   And Jesus said
To make a division
I came myself into this world
So that those who do not see
Should see
And those who see
Should become blind

40   Some of the Pharisees who were with
him
Heard this
And said to him

Surely we
We are not blind also?

41   Jesus said to them
If you were blind
You would not have been at fault
But now you say
We see
So your sin remains

10 *The shepherd of the sheep*
1   Of a certainty I say to you
Anyone
Who does not come through the door
Into the sheepfold
Is a thief and a plunderer

2   But the shepherd of the sheep
Comes in through the door
3   For him
It is opened by the gatekeeper
He calls his own sheep
By their names
And the sheep hear his voice
And he leads them out

4   When he has brought out
All those who are his own
He goes in front of them
And the sheep follow him

Because they know his voice
5 They will not follow a stranger
But will flee from him
Because a stranger's voice
They do not know

6 This was the parable
Which Jesus told them
But they did not understand
What he was saying to them

7 Then Jesus said to them again
I
I AM the door for the sheep
8 All those who came before me
Are thieves and plunderers
But the sheep did not hear them

9 I
I AM the door
Anyone who comes in through me
Will be saved
And will go in
And will go out
And find pasture

10 The thief only comes
To steal
And to kill
And to destroy
I myself have come

So that they may have life
And have it all the more

11 I
I AM the shepherd
The rightful one
The real shepherd
Who lays down his soul-bearing life
For the sheep

12 The hired-man
Who is not a shepherd
And where the sheep
Are not his own
Perceives the wolf coming
And leaves the sheep
And flees
And the wolf
Seizes and scatters them
13 He flees
Because he is a hired-man
And the sheep
Are not in his care

14 I
I AM the shepherd
The real one
I am aware of my own
And those who are mine
Are aware of me
15 As the Father is aware of me

And I myself am aware of the Father
And I lay down my soul-bearing life
For the sheep

16 And I have other sheep
Which are not of this fold
I must bring them also
And they will hear my voice
And become one flock
With one shepherd

17 Therefore the Father loves me
Because I
I lay down my soul-bearing life
So that I may take it again
18 No one takes it from me
I lay it down myself
I have the authority
To lay it down
And I have the authority
To take it again
This commandment I received
From my Father

19 Because of these words
The Jews were again divided
20 And many of them said
He has a demon
And he raves
Why do you hear him?

21 Others said
>> These are not the words
>> Of one possessed by a demon
>> Surely a demon
>> Cannot open the eyes of the blind

The Feast of the Dedication of the Temple

22 In Jerusalem
It was the Festival of the Dedication
23 And it was winter

Jesus walked in the Temple
In Solomon's colonnade

24 There the Jews surrounded him
And said
>> For how long
>> Will you keep our souls in suspense
>> If you are the Christ
>> Tell us so openly

25 Jesus answered them
>> I have told you
>> And you do not believe
>> The deeds that I myself am doing
>> In my Father's name
>> Bear witness to me
26 >> But you
>> You do not believe
>> Because you are not among my sheep

27   My sheep hear my voice
      And I myself am aware of them
      And they follow me
28   And I
      I give them life
      Throughout the ages
      And throughout the ages
      They shall not be destroyed
      And no one shall seize them
      Out of my hand

29   My Father
      Who has given them to me
      Is greater than all
      And no one has power to seize them
      Out of my Father's hand
30   I and my Father are one

31 The Jews took up stones again
    In order to stone him

32   Jesus answered them
      I showed you
      Many of the Father's noble deeds
      For which deed
      Do you stone me?

33   The Jews replied
      It is not for a noble deed
      That we stone you
      But for blasphemy

And because you
Who are a man
Make yourself God

34   Jesus answered
Is it not written in your Law
I
I said
You are gods?

35   If he called those gods
With whom was the word of God
And the Scripture
Cannot be put aside
36   Do you yourselves say
To the one whom the Father has
    consecrated
And sent into the world
You are blaspheming
Because I said
I am the Son of God?

37   If I were not doing my Father's
    deeds
You should not believe me
38   But if I am doing them
Even if you do not believe me
Believe in the deeds
So that you may understand
And continue understanding
That the Father is in me

And I
I am in the Father

39   Again they tried to arrest him
But he went away
From out of their hands

Jesus returns to the Jordan Valley
40   Then he departed again
Across the Jordan
To the place where John
Had been baptizing at first
And he remained there

41   Many people came to him
And they said
John did not perform any signs
But all that John said about this one
Was true

42   And many of those who were there
Believed in him

11 *The raising of Lazarus*
1   Now there was one who was sick
Lazarus of Bethany
The village of Mary
And her sister Martha
2   It was the same Mary
Who anointed the Lord with ointment

And wiped his feet with her hair
Whose brother Lazarus was sick

3   So the sisters sent to Jesus
      And said
          Lord
          You should know
          That he who is your friend
          Is sick

4   When he heard it
      Jesus said
          This sickness
          Does not lead to death
          But is to reveal the glory of God
          That by this means
          The glory of the Son of God may be
             revealed

5 Now Jesus loved Martha
And her sister
And Lazarus
6 But when he heard that he was sick
He remained where he was
For two days
7   Then he said to the disciples
          Let us go to Judea again

8   The disciples said to him
          Rabbi
          Just recently

The Jews were trying to stone you
And now
Will you go there again?

9   Jesus answered
Are there not twelve hours of the day?
If anyone walks in the day
He does not stumble
Because he sees the light of this world
10   But if anyone walks in the night
He stumbles
Because the light is not in him

11   After saying this
He then said to them
Our friend Lazarus
Has fallen asleep
But I am going so that I may awaken
him

12   So the disciples said to him
Lord
If he has fallen asleep
He will be saved

13   Now Jesus had spoken of his death
But they thought
That he spoke of the sleep of rest

14   Therefore Jesus told them plainly
Lazarus has died

15   And for your sakes
I rejoice that I was not there
So that you may believe
But let us go to him

16   Then Thomas
Called the Twin
Said to his fellow disciples
    Let us go
    So that we may also die with him

17   When he came
Jesus found that Lazarus
Had already been in the tomb
Four days

18   Now Bethany
Was near Jerusalem
At a distance of about fifteen stadia
19   And many of the Jews
Had come to Martha and Mary
To console them about their brother

20   When Martha heard
That Jesus was coming
She went to meet him
But Mary still sat in the house

21   Then Martha said to Jesus
    Lord
    If you had been here

This brother of mine
Would not have died
22 And even now I know
That whatever you ask from God
Will be given to you by God

23 Jesus said to her
Your brother will rise

24 Martha said to him
I know that he will rise
In the resurrection
At the most distant day

25 Jesus said to her
I
I AM the resurrection
And the life
He who believes in me
Will live
Even if he dies
26 And all those who live
And believe in me
They will not die
Not unto the ending of the age
Do you believe this?

27 She said to him
Yes Lord
I
I have believed

That you are the Christ
The Son of God
Who is coming into the world

28 After having said this
She went away
   And called her sister Mary
   Saying secretly
      The Teacher has arrived
      And is asking for you

29 When she heard that
She got up quickly
And came to him

30 Now Jesus
Had not come as far as the village
But was still in the place
Where Martha had met him

31 Then the Jews
Who were consoling Mary in the house
When they saw that she got up quickly
And went out
Followed her
Because they thought
She is going to the tomb
To weep there

32   So when Mary
     Came to where Jesus was
     And saw him
     She fell at his feet
          Saying to him
               Lord
               If you had been here
               My brother
               Would not have died

33   Then Jesus
     When he saw her weeping
     And the Jews weeping
     Who had come with her
     Groaned in the spirit
     And was troubled in himself
34   And said
               Where have you laid him?

          They said to him
               Lord
               Come and see

35   Jesus shed tears
36   Therefore the Jews said
               See how he cared for his friend
37   As he had power to open the eyes
               Of a person who was blind
               Could he not have prevented
               This one from dying?

38 Then Jesus
Again groaning in himself
Came to the tomb
It was a cave
And a stone was lying on it

39   Jesus said
        Take up the stone

    Martha
    Sister of the one who had died
    Said to him
        Lord
        By now he stinks
        Because it is the fourth day

40   Jesus said to her
        Did I not tell you
        That if you believe
        You will have sight
        Of the glory of God

41 Then they took up the stone

    Jesus lifted up his eyes
    And said
        Father
        I thank thee
        That thou hast heard me
42   Because I
        I know that thou hearest me always

> But I said this
> For the sake of the crowd standing
>   round
> So that they may believe
> That thou didst send me

43 When he had said this
> He cried with a loud voice
>   Lazarus
>   Come out

44 He who had died
> Came out
> His feet and his hands
> Bound with bandages
> And his face
> Bound round with a cloth

> Jesus said to them
>   Unbind him
>   And let him go

The chief priests and Pharisees hold a council
45 Many of the Jews
> Who had come to Mary
> And who beheld what he did
> Believed in him
46 But some of them went to the Pharisees
> And told them
> What it was that Jesus was doing

47 Then the chief priests and the Pharisees
Assembled a council
And said
> What shall we do?
> Because this man performs many signs
48 If we leave him alone
> Everyone will believe in him
> And the Romans will come
> And will take away
> Both our land
> And our nation

49 But Caiaphas
Who was one of them
And high priest that year
Said to them
> You
> You know nothing
50 Nor do you consider
> That it is better for us
> That one man
> Should die for the people
> And not all the nation perish

51 He did not say this out of himself
But being high priest that year
He prophesied that Jesus
Was about to die for the nation
52 And not only for the nation
But to gather into one
The scattered children of God

53   Therefore from that day onwards
They discussed
How they could bring about his death

54   It was for this reason that Jesus
No longer went about openly
Among the Jews
But went away
Into the country on the edge of the desert
To a town called Ephraim
And stayed there
With his disciples

The last Passover is near

55   Now the Jewish Passover was near
And many people out of the country
Went up to Jerusalem before the Passover

56   There they looked for Jesus
    And said to one another
    As they stood in the Temple
      What do you think?
      Is it certain
      That he will not come to the festival?

57   For the chief priests and the Pharisees
Had given orders
That anyone who knew where he was
Should inform them
So that they could arrest him

12   *The anointing at Bethany*

1   Then six days before the Passover
       Jesus came to Bethany
       The home of Lazarus
       Whom Jesus
       Had raised from the dead

2   There they made a supper for him
       And Martha served
       But Lazarus
       Was one of those
       Who sat at the table with him

3   Then Mary
       Took a pound of costly ointment
       It was pure nard
       And she anointed Jesus' feet
       And with her hair
       She wiped his feet
       And the house was filled
       With the sweet smell of the ointment

4   But one of his disciples said
           (It was Judas Iscariot
           Who was about to betray him)
5   Why was this ointment not sold
               For three hundred denarii
               And given to the poor?

6   He did not say this
       Because the poor mattered to him

But because he was a thief
And took what went into the purse
Which he carried

7 Therefore Jesus said
    Leave her
    So that she may keep it
    For the day of my burial
8   You always have the poor with you
    But you do not always have me

9 When they discovered where he was
   Many of the Jews came there
   And not only because of Jesus
   But also to see Lazarus
   Whom he had raised from the dead

10 Then the chief priests in council
   Decided to kill Lazarus also
11 Because for his sake
   Many of the Jews left
   And believed in Jesus

The entry into Jerusalem
12 The next day
   The crowds coming to the festival
   Heard that Jesus
   Was on his way to Jerusalem
13 And they took branches
   From the palm trees
   And went out to meet him

And they called out
> *Blessed is the King of Israel*
> *Who comes in the name of the Lord*

14   Then Jesus found a young ass
And sat upon it
As it is written
15   *Do not be afraid*
Daughter of Zion
Look how your King is coming
Sitting on the foal of an ass

16   At first
His disciples did not understand
But when Jesus' glory was revealed
Then they remembered
How everything
That had been written about him
Had indeed been done to him

17   The people bore witness
Because they had been with him
When he called Lazarus
Out of the tomb
And raised him from the dead
18   And the crowd met him
Because they had heard
How he had performed this sign

19   Then the Pharisees
Said to one another
    See how helpless you are
    Look how the world
    Has gone after him

Jesus foretells his death

20   Now among those
Who were going up
To worship at the festival
There were some Greeks

21   They came to Philip
Who was from Bethsaida in Galilee
    And said to him
        Sir
        We wish to see Jesus

22   Philip went and told Andrew
And Andrew and Philip
Went and told Jesus

23   Jesus answered them
    The hour has come
    When the glory of the Son of Man
    Is revealed

24   Of a certainty I say to you
    Unless the grain of wheat
    Which falls into the earth
    Dies

It remains alone
But if it dies
It bears fruit in plenty

25 He who cares
About his soul-bearing life
Loses it
And he who hates
His soul-bearing life
In this world
Will keep it living
Throughout the ages

26 If anyone serves me
Let him follow me
And where I
I am
There he who serves me
Will be also
If any one serves me
The Father
Will honour him

27 Now the life of my soul
Has been troubled
And what shall I say?
Father
Save me from this hour?
But therefore I came to this hour
28 Father
Reveal the glory of thy name

Then a voice came from heaven
I have revealed it
And I will reveal it again

29 When the crowd standing there
Heard it
They said
It thundered

Others said
An angel has spoken to him

30 Jesus answered them
This voice was not heard
For my sake
But for yours

31 Now crisis
Has come upon this world
Now the ruler of this world
Will be cast right out
32 And if I
I am lifted up from the earth
I will draw every one to me

33 He said this
To give a sign
As to the way he would die

34 Then the crowd answered him
We have heard from the Law

That the Christ
Remains until the end of the age
How can you say
That the Son of Man
Must be lifted up?
Who is this Son of Man?

35   Then Jesus said to them
For a short time
The light will still be with you
Walk while you have the light
So that darkness
Does not overtake you
Because whoever walks in darkness
Does not know where he is going
36   While you have the light
Believe in the light
So that you may become sons of light

Jesus said this
And going away
He hid himself from them

The Jews are unable to believe
37   Even though he had performed many signs
In their presence
They did not believe in him

38   This was to fulfil the word
Of Isaiah the prophet
When he said

Lord
Who has believed our report?
And to whom has the arm of the Lord
Been made plain?

39 They were not able to believe
    Because again Isaiah said
40 *He has blinded their eyes*
    And hardened their heart
    So that they should not see with the eyes
    And comprehend with the heart
    And turn
    And I will heal them

41 This was said by Isaiah
    Because he saw the glory of his revelation
    And spoke of him

42 Nevertheless
    Even among the rulers
    There were many who believed in him
    But they did not acknowledge it
    Because of the Pharisees
    Who might exclude them from the synagogue

43 For indeed
    They loved the respect of men
    More than the glory of God

44   But Jesus cried out
            Whoever believes in me

Does not believe in me
But in the one who sent me
45   And whoever looks on me
Looks on the one who sent me

46   I
I have come
As light into the world
So that all who believe in me
May not remain in darkness

47   If any one hears my words
And does not keep them
I myself do not act as his judge
Because I did not come
To condemn the world
But to save the world
48   Whoever rejects me
And does not receive my words
Has a judge already
For at the end of time
He will be judged
By the word which I have spoken

49   Because I
I did not speak out of myself
But the Father
Who has sent me
Has given me commandment
As to what I may say
And how I may speak

50   And I know
        That his commandment
        Is life
        Throughout the ages
        Therefore what I
        I say
        I speak as the Father
        Has told me

13   *Jesus washes his disciples' feet*

1   Before the festival of the Passover
        When Jesus knew
        That the hour had come
        When he should pass from this world
        To the Father
        He loved those who were his own
        In the world
        And he loved them to the last

2   During supper
        When already the devil
        Had put the intention to betray him
        Into the heart of Judas Iscariot
        The son of Simon

3   And when Jesus knew
        That everything had been given into his hands
        By the Father
        And that he came forth from God
        And was going to God

4   He rose from supper
And when he had taken off his clothes
He took a towel
And tied it round his waist

5   Then he poured water into a basin
And began to wash the feet
Of the disciples
And to wipe them with the towel
Which he had tied round him

6   He came to Simon Peter
Who said to him
    Lord
    Are you going to wash my feet?

7   Jesus answered him
    Now you do not know
    What I
    I am doing
    But after this you will understand

8   Peter said to him
    As long as this age shall last
    You shall not wash my feet

Jesus answered him
    Unless I wash you
    You have no part with me

9   Simon Peter said to him
    Lord

Not only my feet
But also my hands
And my head

10   Jesus said to him
Anyone who has taken a bath
Has no need to wash
[Except for his feet]
You are clean
But not all of you

11   He said
Not all of you are clean
Because he knew
Who was going to betray him

12   When he had washed their feet
And had put on his clothes
He sat down again
And said to them
Do you understand
What I have done to you?
13   You call me
The Teacher and the Lord
And that is right
For so I am

14   If I have myself washed your feet
Who am Lord and Teacher
You too should wash one another's
feet

15 Because I have given you an example
That as I
I have done to you
You yourselves should do also

16 Of a certainty I say to you
A servant
Is not greater than his master
Nor a messenger
Greater than the one who has sent him
17 If you know this
Blessings will be yours
If you do it

18 I am not speaking about you all
Myself I know
Whom I have chosen
In order that the Scripture may be
fulfilled
Which says
He who eats my bread
Has lifted up his heel against me

19 From now on I shall be telling you
Before it takes place
So that when it does take place
You may believe that
I
I AM

20   Of a certainty I say to you
          He who receives whomever I may
             send
          Receives me
          And he who receives me
          Receives the one who sent me

Judas leaves the upper room

21 When he had said this
Jesus was disturbed in his spirit
     And declared
          Of a certainty I say to you
          One of you will betray me

22 The disciples looked at one another
At a loss as to whom he meant

23 One of the disciples
The one whom Jesus loved
Was leaning on his breast
24   So Simon Peter beckoned to him and said
          Tell us whom he means

25 So leaning back on the breast of Jesus
     He said to him
          Lord
          Who is it?

26   Jesus answered
          It is the one

Where I shall myself dip the portion in
the dish
And shall give it to him

Then he dipped the portion
And took it
And gave it to Judas
Son of Simon Iscariot

27   After the portion
Satan entered into him
    Therefore Jesus said to him
      What you intend to do
      Do quickly

28   But no one sitting there
Understood what he said to him
29   For some thought
Because Judas had the purse
That Jesus had said to him
Buy what we need for the festival
Or that he should give something to the poor

30   Having taken the portion
He went out immediately
And it was night

Jesus begins his farewell talks
31   When he had gone out
    Jesus said
      Now the glory of the Son of Man

Was revealed
And the glory of God
Was revealed in him
32   If the glory of God
Was revealed in him
God will both reveal his glory in him
And will reveal his glory immediately

33   Children
I shall still be with you
For a little while
Then you will search for me
And as I said to the Jews
Where I
I am going
You yourselves have not the power to
   come
So now I am also saying it to you

34   I am giving you a new commandment
That you love one another
Just as I have loved you
You also love one another
35   And because you love one another
Everyone will recognize you
As my disciples

36   Simon Peter said to him
Lord
Where are you going?

Jesus answered
>Where I am going
>You have no power to follow me now
>But you will follow me later

37 Peter said to him
>Lord
>Why am I powerless to follow you
>>just now?
>For you
>I will lay down my soul-bearing life

38 Jesus answered
>Will you lay down your soul-bearing
>>life
>For me?

>Of a certainty I say to you
>A cock will not crow
>Before you have denied me
>Three times

14 *The way, the truth, and the life*
1 Do not let your hearts be troubled
>You believe in God
>You also believe in me

2 There are many rooms
>In my Father's house

If it were not so
Would I have told you
That I am going
To prepare a place for you?

3   And if I go
And prepare a place for you
I will come again
And will take you to myself
So that where I
I am
You indeed may be also
And where I
I am going
You know the way

5   Thomas said to him
Lord
We do not know
Where you are going
How do we know the way?

6   Jesus said to him
I
I AM the way
And the truth
And the life

No one comes to the Father
Except through me
7   If you had recognized me

You would also have known my
  Father
From now on you recognize him
And have seen him

8   Philip said to him
       Lord
       Show us the Father
       And it is enough for us

9   Jesus said to him
       Have I been with you all
       For such a long time
       And you have not recognized me
       Philip?
       He who has seen me
       Has seen the Father
       How can you say
       Show us the Father?
10   Do you not believe
       That I am in the Father
       And that the Father
       Is in me?

       Indeed the words which I say to you
       I do not speak out of myself
       But the Father
       Who remains in me
       Does his deeds
11   Believe me
       I in the Father

And the Father in me
Or believe
For the sake of the deeds themselves

12   Of a certainty I say to you
He who believes in me
Will also do the deeds which I do
    myself
And he will do even greater things
Because I
I am going to the Father

13   Whatever you ask in my name
This I will do
So that the glory of the Father
May be revealed in the Son
14   If you ask anything in my name
I myself will do it

15   If you love me
You will keep my commandments
16   And I myself will ask the Father
And he will give you another
    counsellor
To be with you
Throughout the ages

17   The Spirit of Truth
Whom the world has no power to
    receive
Because it neither perceives him

Nor recognizes him
You recognize him
Because he remains with you
And will be in you

18 I will not leave you orphans
I will come to you

19 There is still a little while
Then the world
Will lose sight of me
But you will not lose sight of me
And because I
I live
You yourselves will live also

20 In that day
It will become clear to you
I in my Father
And you in me
And I in you

21 He who has my commandments
And keeps them
Is the one who loves me
And he who loves me
Will be loved by my Father
And I
I will love him
And will make myself visible to him

22   Judas (not Iscariot) said to him
            Lord
            What has taken place
            So that you will make yourself visible
                to us
            And not to the world?

23   Jesus answered him
            If anyone loves me
            He will keep my word
            And my Father will love him
            And we will come to him
            And make our dwelling with him
24   Anyone who does not love me
            Does not keep my words
            And the word which you hear
            Is not mine
            But is from the Father
            Who sent me

25   I have said this to you
            While remaining with you
26   But the Counsellor
            The Holy Spirit
            Whom the Father
            Will send in my name
            Will teach you everything
            And recall to you everything
            Which I myself have told you

27
Peace I leave with you
My peace I give to you
Not as the world makes a gift
I
I give to you

Do not let your hearts be troubled
Nor let them be fearful
28
You heard what I told you myself
I am going away
But I will come back to you
If you loved me
You would have rejoiced
Because I am going to the Father
For the Father
Is greater than I

29
And now I have told you
Before it takes place
So that when it takes place
You may believe

30
I will no longer say much to you
Because the ruler of this world
Is coming
And he has no part in me
31
For the world's understanding
Of my love for the Father
Whatever the Father has commanded
      me
That is what I do

Rise
Let us go from here

15 *The true vine*

1   I
    I AM the true vine
    And my Father cultivates the ground

2   He takes away every branch of mine
    That bears no fruit
    And cleans every fruit-bearing branch
    To make it bear more fruit

3   You are clean already
    Because of the word
    Which I have spoken to you

4   Remain in me
    And I in you
    As the branch has no power to bear
     fruit
    Unless it remains in the vine
    Neither have you
    Unless you remain in me

5   I
    I AM the vine
    You are the branches
    He who remains in me
    And I in him
    Bears plentiful fruit
    Because separated from me
    You have no power to do anything

6   Those who do not remain in me
     Are like branches which dry up
     They are gathered together
     Thrown into the fire
     And burnt

7   If you remain in me
     And my words remain in you
     Ask whatever you will
     And it shall come about for you

8   My Father's glory is revealed
     When you bear plentiful fruit
     And so become my disciples

9   As the Father has loved me
     I
     I have also loved you
     Remain in my love

10   If you keep my commandments
     You will remain in my love
     As I
     I have kept my Father's commandments
     And remain in his love

11   I have said this to you
     So that my joy may be in you
     And that your joy may be complete

12   This is my commandment
     That you love one another
     As I have loved you

13   No one can have greater love
Than to lay down his soul-bearing life
For his friends

14   You are my friends
If you do
What I myself command you

15   I no longer call you servants
Because the servant
Does not know
What his master is doing
But I have proclaimed you friends
Because all that I heard from my
    Father
I have passed on to you

16   You did not choose me
But I
I have chosen you
So that you yourselves should go and
    bear fruit
And your fruit should remain
Then whatever you ask the Father
In my name
He will give you

17   This is what I command you
To love one another

Hatred and persecution

18   If the world hates you
        You are aware
        That it has hated me before you
19   If you belonged to the world
        The world would have cared for its own
        But because you do not belong to the
            world
        I
        I chose you out of the world
        Therefore the world hates you

20   Remember what I myself said to you
        The servant is not greater than his
            master
        If they persecuted me
        They will also persecute you
        If they kept my word
        They will also keep yours
21   But they will do all this to you
        Because of my name
        As they do not know
        The one who sent me

22   If I had not come
        And spoken to them
        They would not have been to blame
        But now they have no excuse for their
            sin
23   Anyone who hates me
        Hates my Father also

24   If I had not done deeds among them
Which no one else has done
They would not have been to blame
But now they have seen and have
    hated
Both me and my Father
25   So that the word
Which is written in their Law
Might be fulfilled
They hated me
Without a cause

26   But when the Counsellor comes
Whom I myself will send to you
From the Father
The Spirit of Truth
Who proceeds from the Father
He will be my witness
27   You also are witnesses
Because you have been with me
From the beginning

16   This I have told you
So that you should not be shaken
2   They will exclude you from
    synagogue
Indeed the hour is coming
When anyone who kills you
Will think that he is offering a service
    to God

3   And they will do all this because
         They neither recognize the Father
         Nor me

4   But this I have said to you
         So that when the hour comes
         You may remember that I told you
             myself

The sending of the Holy Spirit
         I did not say this to you
         From the beginning
         Because I was with you
5   Now I am going away
         To the one who sent me
         Yet none of you asks me
         Where are you going?
6   But because of what I have told you
         Sorrow has filled your hearts

7   But I
         I am telling you the truth
         It is better for you
         That I myself should go away
         Because if I do not go away
         Surely the Counsellor
         Will not come to you
         But if I go
         I will send him to you
8   And when he comes
         He will make clear to the world

What is sin
What is right
And what is the judgment

9   What is sin
Because they do not believe in me
10   What is right
Because I am going to the Father
And you will lose sight of me
11   What is the judgment
Because the ruler of this world
Has been condemned

12   I still have much to say to you
But you cannot bear it now

13   When the Spirit of Truth comes
He will guide you into all the truth
He will not speak out of himself
But he will say what he has heard
And will proclaim to you
The things that are to come

14   He will reveal my glory
Because what he receives from me
He will proclaim to you
15   Everything that the Father has
Is mine
Therefore I said
What he receives from me
He will proclaim to you

16   After a little while
        You will lose sight of me
        Then after a little while
        You will see me again

17   Some of his disciples
        Said to one another
            What is he saying to us?
            After a little while
            You will lose sight of me
            Then after a little while
            You will see me again
            And
            Because I am going to the Father?

18   And so they said
            What is he saying?
            After a little while?
            We do not know
            What he is saying

19   Jesus understood that they wished to
            question him
        And he said to them
            Do you consult one another about
                this
            Because I said
            After a little while
            You will lose sight of me
            Then after a little while
            You will see me again?

20
> Of a certainty I say to you
> That you will weep
> And will mourn
> But the world will rejoice
> You will be filled with sorrow
> But your sorrow will turn into joy

21
> A woman in childbirth has suffering
> Because her hour has come
> But once the child is born
> She forgets the distress
> In her joy
> That a man has been born into the
> world

22
> It is now that you have sorrow
> But I will see you again
> And your hearts will rejoice
> And no one
> Will take your joy from you

23
> And in that day
> You will not put any question to me

> Of a certainty I say to you
> Whatever you ask of the Father
> He will give it to you in my name

24
> Until now
> You did not ask anything in my name
> Ask and you will receive
> So that your joy may be complete

25   I have told you all this in parables
The hour is coming
When I will no longer speak to you in
    parables
But quite openly
Will proclaim to you the Father

26   In that day
You will ask in my name
And I do not say to you
That I
I will request the Father for you
27   Because the Father is himself a friend
    to you
As indeed you have been friends to me
And have believed
That I
I came forth from God
28   I came forth out of the Father
And have come into the world
Now I leave the world again
And go to the Father

29   His disciples said to him
We see that you are speaking quite
    openly
And not in parables
30   Now we understand
That you know everything
And do not need anyone to question
    you

Because of this we believe
That you came forth from God

31 Jesus answered them
Do you now believe?
32 See how the hour is coming
Indeed it has come already
When you will be scattered
Each one on his own
And will leave me alone
Yet I am not alone
Because the Father is with me

33 I have told you all this
So that in me
You may have peace
In the world
You will have trouble
But have confidence
I
I have won the victory
Over the world

17 *The high priestly prayer of Christ*
1 When Jesus had spoken
He lifted up his eyes to heaven
Saying
Father
The hour has come
Reveal the glory of thy Son

So that the Son
May reveal thy glory

2   As thou gavest him authority
Over all flesh
So that he may give life
Throughout the ages
To everyone whom thou gavest to him

3   And this is life
Throughout the ages
That they may become aware of thee
The only true God
And the one
Whom thou hast sent out
Jesus Christ

4   I myself revealed thy glory
On the earth
And finished the work
Which thou gavest me to do

5   And now Father
Glorify me with thy self
With the glory which I had with thee
Before the world came into being

6   I showed forth thy name
To the men whom thou gavest me
Out of the world
They belonged to thee
And thou gavest them to me
And they have kept thy word

7   Now it has become clear to them
That all those things
Which thou gavest me
Are from thee
8   Because the teaching
Which thou gavest to me
I have given to them
And they have received it
And are aware
That in truth
I came forth from thee
And they have believed
That thou has sent me out

9   I
I pray for them
I do not pray for the world
But for those whom thou gavest to me
Because they belong to thee
10   All those who are mine
Belong to thee
All those who belong to thee
Are mine
And my glory has been revealed in
    them

11   I am no longer in the world
But they are in the world
And I
I come to thee

Holy Father
Keep in thy name
Those whom thou gavest to me
So that they may be one
As we are

12
When I was with them
I kept in thy name
Those whom thou gavest to me
I guarded them
And none of them was destroyed
Except the son of destruction
That the Scripture
Might be fulfilled

13
But now I come to thee
And I have said all this
In the world
So that in themselves
They may have my joy
To the full

14
I myself gave thy word to them
And the world
Has hated them
Because they do not belong to the
    world
Just as I
I do not belong to the world

15   I do not pray
That thou shouldst take them
Out of the world
But that thou shouldst protect them
From the evil one

16   They do not belong to the world
Just as I
I do not belong to the world
17   Consecrate them in the truth
Thy word is truth
18   As thou hast sent me
Into the world
Even so I
I send them into the world
19   And for them I consecrate myself
So that they also
May be consecrated in truth

20   It is not for these only
That I pray
But also for those
Who will believe in me
Through their word

21   So that they all may be one
As thou
Father
Art in me
And I
I in thee

They also may be in us
And the world may believe
That thou has sent me out

22 The revelation which thou gavest me
I myself gave to them
So that they may be one
As we are one

23 I in them
And thou in me
So that they may be completely one
And the world may be aware
That thou hast sent me out
And hast loved them
As thou hast loved me

24 Father
I will that those whom thou gavest to
    me
May also be with me
Where I
I am
So that they may perceive my glory
Which thou hast given to me
Because thou hast loved me
Before the foundation of the world

25 Righteous Father
The world was not aware of thee
But I

I was aware of thee
And these were aware
That thou hast sent me out
26   And I have declared to them thy name
And will declare it
So that the love
With which thou hast loved me
May be in them
And I
I in them

18 *Jesus is arrested*

1   Having said this
Jesus went forth with his disciples
Across the winter-stream of the Kidron
Where there was a garden
Into which he entered with his disciples

2   Now Judas
Who was betraying him
Knew the place
Because Jesus and his disciples
Often met there

3   So then Judas
Came from the chief priests and the Pharisees
With a band of soldiers and officials
Carrying torches and lamps and weapons

4   Then as Jesus knew everything
That was coming to him

He went forward
    And said to them
        Who are you searching for?

5   They answered him
        Jesus
        The Nazarene

       He said to them
        I
        I AM

Now Judas
Who was betraying him
Stood with them

6   When Jesus said to them
I
I AM
They moved backwards
And fell to the ground

7   Then he questioned them again
        Who are you searching for?

       And they said
        Jesus
        The Nazarene

8   Jesus answered them
        I said to you

That I
I AM
So if you are searching for me
Allow these men to go

9   This was to fulfil the words
Which he had spoken
Of those whom thou gavest me
I have not lost one

10   Then Simon Peter
Who had a sword
Drew it
And struck the high priest's servant
Cutting off his right ear
The servant's name was Malchus

11   So Jesus said to Peter
Put your sword
Into the sheath
Shall I not drink the cup
Which the Father
Has given to me?

Jesus before Annas and Caiaphas

12   Then the band of soldiers
With their captain
And the Jewish officials
Took Jesus
And bound him

13   They led him first to Annas
The father-in-law of Caiaphas
Who was high priest that year

14   Now it was Caiaphas
Who had advised the Jews
That it was better
For one man to die
On behalf of the people

15   Simon Peter
And another disciple
Followed Jesus
That disciple was known to the high priest
And he went with Jesus
Into the high priest's court

16   But Peter
Stood outside at the door
So the other disciple
Who was known to the high priest
Went out
And spoke to the doorkeeper
And brought in Peter

17   But the maidservant
Who kept the door
Said
    Are you not
    Also one of this man's disciples?

He said
I am not

18 The servants and the officials
Having made a charcoal fire
Stood and warmed themselves
Because it was cold
Peter also stood with them
And warmed himself

19 Then the high priest
Questioned Jesus
About his disciples
And about his teaching

20 Jesus answered him
I myself have spoken openly
To the world
Indeed I always taught
In a synagogue
Or in the Temple
Where all the Jews meet together
And I have said nothing in secret
21 Why do you ask me?
Ask the people
Who heard what I said to them
For they are the ones who know
What I
I have said

22 When he had said this
One of the officials
Who stood near by
Gave Jesus a slap on the face
    Saying
        Is this how you answer
        The high priest?

23   But Jesus replied to him
        If what I said was wrong
        Bear witness to the wrong
        But if it was rightly said
        Why do you strike me?

24 Then Annas had him bound
And sent him to Caiaphas
The high priest

25 Now Simon Peter
Was standing there warming himself

    So they said to him
        Are not you
        Also one of his disciples?

    He denied it
    And said
        I am not

26 One of the high priest's servants
Was related to the one

Whose ear Peter had cut off
   And he said
      Did I not see you myself
      In the garden with him?

27   Then Peter denied it again
   And immediately a cock crew

Jesus before Pilate
28   They led Jesus
From Caiaphas
To the praetorium
It was early
And they did not go into the praetorium
So that they should not be defiled
But be able to eat the passover

29   Therefore Pilate
   Went outside to speak to them
   And said
      What accusation
      Do you bring against this man?

30   They answered him
      We would not have handed him over
         to you
      If he had not been doing wrong

31   Pilate said to them
      Take him yourselves
      And judge him according to your law

The Jews replied
    It is not lawful for us
    To condemn anyone to death

32 This was to fulfil the word of Jesus
Which he had spoken
Telling of the death
Which he was about to die

33 Then Pilate
Entered the praetorium again
    And calling Jesus
    He said to him
        Are you
        The King of the Jews?

34 Jesus answered
    Do you say this yourself
    Or have others
    Said this about me?

35 Pilate replied
    Am I myself a Jew?
    Your own countrymen
    And the chief priests
    Handed you over to me
    What have you done?

36 Jesus answered
    My kingdom
    Is not of this world

If my kingdom
Was of this world
My followers would have fought
So that I should not have been handed
over
To the Jews
But my kingdom
Is not here

37   Pilate said to him
Then you are not really a king?

Jesus answered
You say
That I am a king
I myself was born for this
And for this
I have come into the world
To bear witness to the truth
Everyone who belongs to the truth
Hears my voice

38   Pilate said to him
What is truth?

And having said this
He went out again to the Jews
And said to them
I
I do not find him guilty
39   But you have a custom

That at the Passover
One prisoner should be released
Do you choose
That I should release to you
The King of the Jews?

40   Then they cried out again
        Not this one
        But Barabbas

Now Barabbas
Was a bandit

19   Then Pilate
Had Jesus taken away
And scourged
2   The soldiers plaited a crown of thorns
And put it on his head
And they threw a purple garment round
   him

3   They came up to him
     And said
        Hail
        King of the Jews

And they slapped him
On the face

4   Pilate went outside again
     And said to them

Look how I am bringing him out to
    you
So that you may be clear
That I do not find him guilty

5   Then Jesus came out
Wearing the thorny crown
And the purple garment

And he said to them
    Look upon the man

6   When the chief priests
And the guards saw him
    They cried out
        Crucify him
        Crucify him

Pilate said to them
    You take him yourselves
    And crucify him
    Because I
    I do not find him guilty

7   The Jews answered him
    We have a law
    And according to that law
    He ought to die
    Because he made himself
    The Son of God

8   So when Pilate
      Heard these words
      He was still more afraid
9   And went into the praetorium again
           And said to Jesus
                Where do you come from?

      But Jesus
      Did not give him any answer

10   Therefore Pilate said to him
                Will you not speak to me?
                Do you not know
                That I have the authority
                To release you
                And I have the authority
                To crucify you?

11   Jesus answered
                You would have no authority
                Over me
                Unless it was given to you
                From above
                Therefore he
                Who handed me over to you
                Has the greater sin

      Jesus is condemned to death
12   From then on
      Pilate tried to release him

But the Jews cried out
    If you release this one
    You are no friend to Caesar
    Everyone who makes himself a king
    Speaks against Caesar

13 Then Pilate
When he heard these words
Brought Jesus outside
And sat on the judgment seat
In a place called The Pavement
But in Hebrew
Gabbatha

14 Now it was the Preparation of the Passover
At about the sixth hour
    He said to the Jews
        Look upon your king

15 But they shouted
        Take him
        Take him
        Crucify him

Pilate said to them
    Shall I crucify your king?

The chief priests answered
    We have no other king
    Except Caesar

16 Then he handed him over to them
To be crucified

The crucifixion
17 So they took Jesus
And carrying his own cross
He went out
To the place called the Place of a Skull
Or in Hebrew
Golgotha
18 Where they crucified him
And with him two others
One on either side
And Jesus in the centre

19 Pilate wrote an inscription
And had it put on the cross
On it was written
Jesus the Nazarene
The King of the Jews

20 Many of the Jews
Read this inscription
Because the place
Where Jesus was crucified
Was near the city
And it was written
In Hebrew
In Latin
And in Greek

21   Therefore the chief priests of the Jews
    Said to Pilate
      Do not write
      The King of the Jews
      But that he said
      I am King of the Jews

22   Pilate answered
      What I have written
      I have written

23   When the soldiers
   Had crucified Jesus
   They took his clothing
   And made four shares
   A share for each soldier

   There was also the tunic
   Now the tunic had no seam
   But was woven in one piece
24   So they said to one another
      Do not let us tear it
      But cast lots
      To see who should have it

   This is in order that the Scripture
   Might be fulfilled
   They parted my clothing
   Among themselves
   And over my clothes
   They cast a lot

25   And this
Is what the soldiers did

But beside Jesus' cross
Stood his mother
And his mother's sister
Mary the wife of Clopas
And Mary Magdalene

26   When Jesus saw his mother
And the disciple whom he loved
Standing there
    He said to his mother
      Here is your son

27   Then he said to the disciple
      Here is your mother

And from that hour
The disciple
Took her into his home

28   After this
When Jesus knew
That everything was finished
In order that the Scripture
Might be fulfilled
    He said
      I thirst

29   A jar full of vinegar
Was standing there
So they put a sponge full of vinegar
On to hyssop
And brought it to his mouth

30   When he had taken the vinegar
Jesus said
It is finished

And he bowed his head
And delivered up his spirit

31   As it was the Preparation
And the Jews
Did not want the bodies
To remain on the cross
On the sabbath
Because that sabbath
Was a great day
They requested Pilate
To allow their legs to be broken
And to allow them to be taken away

The burial

32   So the soldiers came
And broke the first one's legs
Then those of the other one
Who was crucified with him

33 When they came to Jesus
And saw that he had already died
They did not break his legs
34 But one of the soldiers
Pierced his side with a lance
And blood and water
Came out immediately

35 He has borne witness
Who saw this
And his witness is true
And he knows
That he speaks the truth
So that you also may believe

36 For all this took place
In order that the Scripture
Might be fulfilled
No bone of him
Shall be broken

37 And again
Another Scripture says
They shall look on him
Whom they pierced

38 Now after all this
Joseph of Arimathea
Who was a disciple of Jesus
But had kept it secret
For fear of the Jews

Asked Pilate
If he might take the body of Jesus
And Pilate gave him leave

39 Nicodemus
Who had first come to Jesus at night
Came with him
And he brought a mixture of myrrh and aloes
Weighing about a hundred pounds

40 So they took Jesus' body
And bound it in linen sheets
With the spices
According to the burial custom of the Jews

41 In the place where he was crucified
There was a garden
And in the garden
A new tomb
In which no one
Had yet been laid

42 Because for the Jews
It was the Preparation
And because the tomb
Was near by
They laid Jesus there

20 *Mary Magdalene and two disciples find the tomb empty*
1 On the first day after the sabbath
Mary Magdalene

Came to the tomb
It was early in the morning
And still dark

She saw that the stone
Had been taken from the tomb
2   So she ran
And came to Simon Peter
And to the other disciple
The one dear to Jesus

And she said to them
They have taken the Lord
Out of the tomb
And we do not know
Where they have laid him

3   Then Peter
And the other disciple
Went out and came to the tomb

4   Now the two ran together
And the other disciple
Ran faster than Peter
And came to the tomb first
5   When he stooped down
He saw the linen clothes lying there
But he did not go in

6   Simon Peter followed him
And went into the tomb

And he perceived the linen sheets
7   And the napkin
Which was on his head
Not lying with the linen sheets
But rolled up separately
In a place by itself

8   Then the other disciple
The one who had come to the tomb first
Went in
And he saw and believed

9   Because they did not yet know
The Scripture which said
That he should rise from the dead

10   Then the disciples
Went away to their home

Jesus appears to Mary Magdalene
11   But Mary
Stood outside the tomb
She was weeping
And as she wept
She bent down into the tomb
12   And perceived two angels in white
One was sitting at the head
And one at the feet
Where the body of Jesus
Had been lying

13   They said to her
      Woman
      Why are you weeping?

    She said to them
      Because they have taken my Lord
      And I do not know
      Where they have laid him

14   Having said this
She turned back
And perceived Jesus
Standing there
But she did not know
That it was Jesus

15   Jesus said to her
      Woman
      Why are you weeping?
      For whom are you searching?

    She thought he was the gardener
    And she said to him
      Sir
      If you have taken him away
      Tell me where you have laid him
      And I will take him

16   Jesus said to her
      Mary

174

She turned
And said to him in Hebrew
    Rabboni
    Which means teacher

17   Jesus said to her
        Do not touch me
        Because I have not yet ascended
        To the Father

        But go to my brothers
        And tell them
        That I am ascending
        To my Father
        And to your Father
        And to my God
        And to your God

18   Mary Magdalene
Came to the disciples
And brought the news
    Saying to them
        I have seen the Lord

And she told them
What he had said to her

Jesus appears to the disciples in the upper room
19   On that day
The first after the sabbath
In the early evening

When the disciples were behind closed doors
For fear of the Jews
Jesus came
And stood among them
    And said
        Peace be with you

20   And having said this
He showed them
Both his hands
And his side

Then the disciples rejoiced
On seeing the Lord

21   Jesus said to them again
           Peace be with you
           As the Father has sent me
           I also send you

22   And having said this
He breathed on them
    And said
        Receive Holy Spirit
23   Those whom you free from their sins
        They are freed from them
        Those whom you hold to them
        They are held

24   But Thomas
One of the twelve
Called the Twin
Was not with them when Jesus came

25   So the other disciples
Said to him
    We have seen the Lord

      But he said to them
    Unless I see in his hands
    The mark of the nails
    And put my finger
    Into the place of the nails
    And put my hand
    Into his side
    I will not believe

26   And after eight days
His disciples were again inside
And Thomas was with them
The doors were closed
But Jesus came
And stood among them
    And said
      Peace be with you

27   Then he said to Thomas
    Bring your finger here
    And look on my hands
    And bring your hand

And put it into my side
And be not unbelieving
But believe

28 Thomas answered him
My Lord and my God

29 Jesus said to him
Have you believed
Because you have seen me?
Blessed are they
Who do not see
And yet believe

30 Now Jesus performed many other signs
In the presence of his disciples
Which have not been recorded in this book
31 But these have been recorded
So that you may believe
That Jesus is the Christ
The Son of God
And that in believing
You may have life
In his name

21 *The appearance by the Sea of Tiberias*
1 Afterwards
Jesus showed himself
To his disciples again
By the Sea of Tiberias

And he showed himself
In this way

2   Simon Peter
Was together with Thomas
Called the Twin
Nathanael from Cana in Galilee
The sons of Zebedee
And two other disciples

3   Simon Peter said to the others
I am going fishing

They said to him
And we are coming with you

They went out
And embarked in the boat
And during that night
They caught nothing

4   When dawn came
Jesus stood on the shore
Although the disciples
Did not know
That it was Jesus

5   Jesus said to them
Children
Have you no fish to eat?

They answered
   No

6   So he said to them
      Cast the net
      On the right side of the boat
      And you will find some

Then they cast it
And were no longer able to haul it in
Because of the full catch of fish
7   Then the disciple whom Jesus loved
      Said to Peter
        It is the Lord

When Simon Peter
Heard it is the Lord
He tied his tunic round him
Because he was naked
And threw himself into the sea
8   But the other disciples
Came in the little boat
Dragging the net with the fish
As they were not far from the land
Only about two hundred cubits

9   When they disembarked
On to the land
They saw a charcoal fire there
With a fish lying on it
And bread

10   Jesus said to them
                Bring some of the fish
                Which you have just caught

11   Simon Peter went on board
        And drew the net to the land
        It was full of large fishes
        A hundred and fifty-three
        And even with so many
        The net was not torn

12   Jesus said to them
                Come
                Make an early meal

        None of the disciples
        Ventured to ask the question
        Who indeed are you?
        They knew
        It is the Lord

13   Jesus came
        And took bread
        And gave it to them
        And also the fish

14   Now this was the third time
        That Jesus
        Showed himself to his disciples
        After being raised from the dead

The charge to Peter

15 When they had made their meal
    Jesus said to Simon Peter
        Simon
        Son of John
        Do you love me more than these do?

    He replied
        Yes Lord
        You know
        That you are dear to me

    Jesus said to him
        Feed my little lambs

16   Then he said to him again
    The second time
        Simon
        Son of John
        Do you love me?

    He replied
        Yes Lord
        You know
        That you are dear to me

    Jesus said to him
        Shepherd my little sheep

17   Then he said to him
    For the third time
        Simon

Son of John
Am I dear to you?

Peter was grieved
That he said to him
The third time
Am I dear to you?

And he said to him
Lord
You know everything
You are aware
That you are dear to me

Jesus said to him
Feed my little sheep

18   Of a certainty I say to you
When you were young
You tied your own belt
And walked where you wished
But when you grow old
You will stretch out your hands
And someone else will tie you
And will carry you
Where you do not wish to go

19   And he said this
To show by what death
He will reveal
The glory of God

When he had told him this
He said to him
    Follow me

20   Peter turned
And he saw that the disciple whom Jesus
    loved
Was following
He was the one
Who had leaned on his breast at the supper
And had said
Lord
Who will betray you?

21   When he saw him
Peter said to Jesus
    Lord
        What about this one?

22   Jesus said to him
    If it is my will
    For him to remain until I come
    Does that concern you?
    You follow me

23   Because of this
It was said among the brothers
That the disciple would not die
But Jesus did not say
That he would not die
But said

If it is my will
For him to remain until I come
Does that concern you?

Conclusion

24 This is the disciple
Who bears witness to these events
And who has recorded them
And we know
That what he says is true

25 Jesus also did many other things
Indeed if they were all written down
I expect that the world itself
Would not contain
The books being written

References

1:23 Isa.40:3
2:17 Ps.69:9
6:31 Ps.78:24
6:45 Isa.54:13
7:38 Obscure. The words
      may come from the
      liturgy of the Feast of
      Tabernacles.
10:34 Ps.82:6
12:13 Ps.118:26

12:15 Zech.9:9
12:38 Isa.53:1
12:40 Isa.6:9--10
13:18 Ps.41:9
15:25 Ps.35:19, 69:4
18:9 John 17:12
19:24 Ps.22:18
19:36 Exod.12:46, Ps.34:20
19:37 Zech. 12:10

Galatians
Ephesians
Philippians
Colossians
The Letters of Paul

*A new translation edited
by Stanley Drake*

This translation of the shorter letters is an attempt to come nearer to Paul's original intention. The grandeur of Paul's message begins to address us with all its fiery potency as the translators seek to create a fullness of expression for it out of a modern consciousness.

'In our own time we are seeking a Christianity which can meet our aspirations for individual development and freedom. Our starting-point is our own experience and not a revelation mediated by the Church. Paul was fortunate that the source of his work lay in a revelation that was also a direct experience. This enabled him to grasp that the essential of Christianity is the relationship of the individual to Christ through faith.'

(From the Introduction to Galatians by Michael Tapp)

Floris Books